tennis's new wave

Venus & Serena
Williams

Sisters in Arms

By
Mark Stewart

THE MILLBROOK PRESS
BROOKFIELD, CONNECTICUT

M

THE MILLBROOK PRESS

Produced by
BITTERSWEET PUBLISHING
John Sammis, President
and
TEAM STEWART, INC.

Series Design and Electronic Page Makeup by
JAFFE ENTERPRISES
Ron Jaffe

Researched and Edited by Mike Kennedy

All photos courtesy
AP/ Wide World Photos, Inc.
except the following:
SportsChrome USA: Martin Rose, photographer — Cover
June Harrison — Pages 6 (© 1978), 7 (© 1998), 13 (© 1995), 15 (© 1992),
16 (© 1985), 18 bottom right (© 1999), 20 (© 1998), 22 bottom right (© 1995),
23 (© 1997), 24 bottom right (© 1997), 25 (© 1997), 27 (© 1998), 28 top left (© 1998),
28 bottom right (© 1999), 32 (© 1998), 34 (© 1999), 35 (© 1999), 37 (© 1999),
38 (© 1999), 39 top left (© 1999), 39 bottom right (© 1999), 41 (© 1999),
42 (© 1995), 44 (© 1999), 45 (© 1999)
The following images are from the collection of Team Stewart:
Time Inc. — Pages 10 (© 2000), 30 (© 1998), 33 top right (© 1998),
33 bottom left (© 1999)

Published by
The Millbrook Press, Inc.
2 Old New Milford Road
Brookfield, Connecticut   06804

http://www.millbrookpress.com

Library of Congress Cataloging-in-Publication Data

Stewart, Mark.
 Venus & Serena Williams: sisters in arms / by Mark Stewart
 p.   cm.   — (Tennis's new wave)
 Includes index.
 Summary: Describes the lives of two African-American sisters who stunned the professional tennis
world with their rapid rise to the top.
 ISBN 0-7613-1803-8 (lib. bdg.)
 1. Williams, Venus, 1980– —Juvenile literature. 2. Williams, Serena, 1981– —Juvenile literature.
3. Tennis players—United States—Biography—Juvenile literature. 4. Afro-American women tennis
players —Biography—Juvenile literature [1. Williams, Venus, 1980– 2. Williams, Serena, 1981–
3. Tennis players 4. Afro-Americans—Biography. 5. Women—Biography.] I. Title: Venus and Serena
Williams. II. Title. III. Series.
GV994.W49 S74 2000
796.342'092'273--dc21
 [B]   00-024921

1 3 5 7 9 10 8 6 4 2

Contents

Where Dreams Go to Die

chapter 1

"It was a suburban ghetto."
— ORACENE WILLIAMS

Dreams die hard in South Central Los Angeles. But that does not stop the dreamers. Richard and Oracene Williams wanted their daughters to rise above the mean streets of Compton, California; they made every sacrifice and gave them everything they could. Things like intelligence, muscle, and desire—and the ability to come back stronger and smarter each time you get knocked to the ground.

Richard Williams wanted five girls, he told his wife when they married in 1972. The couple produced a quintet of lovely daughters: Yetunde, Isha, Lyndrea, Venus, and Serena. To support seven people, both parents worked very hard. Oracene was a private duty nurse, and Richard had his own security company. They were better off than most in Compton, but they were never safe from the growing problems of gangs, drugs, and street crime that were slowly consuming this once-quiet neighborhood.

Venus (left) and Serena Williams have come a long way since their early years in Compton, California. Today, they form the most dynamic duo in professional tennis.

Virginia Ruzici, a Top 20 player in the 1970s, inspired Richard Williams to teach his daughters tennis.

A few years before Venus was born, Richard was clicking through the television channels when he stopped to watch the end of a women's tennis match. He studied a player named Virginia Ruzici as she closed out her opponent and then accepted the tournament's $30,000 champion's check. Richard was in awe. That woman had just made more money in 90 minutes than he would make that entire year!

Richard knew a natural athlete when he saw one, and Ruzici clearly possessed a great gift. But there was nothing extraordinary about how she played. He suspected that the reason she was a high-paid tennis star was that she had been practicing and playing since childhood. At that moment, Richard decided his final two daughters would be tennis stars.

What if they turned out to be boys? Richard would not hear of it—once he set his mind to something, it always got done.

Venus was born in June of 1980. Serena came into the world 15 months later. Their father began collecting all the tennis books and videotapes he could. It was a sport he had never played, so before he taught his daughters, he knew he had to

Did You Know?

Richard Williams grew up in a remote region of Louisiana. He dreamed of playing pro basketball. He quit high school to tour with an all-black basketball team called the Harlem Clowns. Oracene Williams, a graduate of Eastern Michigan University with a degree in education, dreamed of being a singer.

teach himself. When Venus turned four, he presented her with her first racket and drove her over to the public courts. After a few words of advice, Venus was able to pop the ball over the net almost every time.

Tennis has forged an unbreakable bond between Venus and her father.

Venus loved tennis. What she liked best was that it was the one sure way to have her dad all to herself. She had no idea that her father wanted her to become a pro some day. And she had no idea that, in the nearby suburbs of Los Angeles, thousands of girls were learning tennis at country clubs and tennis centers with the finest equipment and training.

From where Venus stood, the cracked courts of Compton and the shabby balls her father tossed her way looked just fine.

Venus Rising

chapter 1

> *"In my heart and mind I don't think anybody's as good as me."*
> — VENUS WILLIAMS

By the age of six, Venus Williams could smack backhands and forehands across the net with great accuracy and consistency. When she and her father were not puttering down to the public courts in his beat-up Volkswagen bus, she would watch tennis videos and live matches on television. Then Venus would go out and imitate the grips the top stars used, and she would try to copy their footwork. She also noticed that the most successful players were the ones who were able to find an opponent's weakness, then keep hitting to the same spot. Venus was beginning to understand that there is a lot of thinking in tennis.

Sitting right next to Venus, soaking up just as much tennis knowledge, was her younger sister, Serena. She wanted so badly to play, and would be heartbroken when Venus and her father left the house for one of their practice sessions. When Serena turned five, she joined them. Soon, the two sisters were blasting away at each other. "It was like nuclear war," Serena remembers.

Young Venus gets encouragement from her mother prior to giving a 1995 tennis clinic in Oakland, California.

When the Williams sisters got in a groove, it was like they were playing in a faraway place where they were all that mattered. They remember those days as being magical. The reality was quite different. During the 1980s, street gangs ruled Compton. There were some places even the police dared not go. Crack cocaine had turned decent people into desperate criminals, and there were more guns in the hands of young people than anyone could ever remember. "We play in hell," Richard Williams often reminded his daughters.

The first trading card picturing both Williams sisters is a favorite among collectors.

Indeed, one of the first lessons Venus and Serena learned was how to lie flat and crawl for cover the instant they heard gunshots. Richard was not going to see his dream ended by a stray bullet. It got so bad that he and Oracene devised ways for the girls to train without leaving the safety of the house. For example, they were probably the only parents who *encouraged* their kids to jump on their beds—it was a perfect way to strengthen the muscles in their legs.

When the Williams sisters were not playing on the courts, they usually could be found playing sports in school. Both girls excelled at everything they tried, including soccer, softball, and gymnastics. Venus was an amazing runner. At the age of eight, she completed a mile in under five-and-a-half minutes. In the classroom, they were just as serious and competitive, bringing home good marks despite overcrowded classrooms and overworked teachers.

Around her 10th birthday, Venus was asked to make a choice. Her parents feared that the more sports she tried, the harder it would be to focus on one—and this might keep her from becoming a world-class athlete. Venus understood what her parents were saying. She chose tennis. Why? "I thought I could be number one," she remembers.

Venus had good reason to be so confident. She had begun entering junior tournaments in the area and was overwhelming the other girls. Venus was aggressive, and even fierce at times. She was taller and stronger and faster than everyone else, and she never got tired. She beat players quickly, hammering at their weaknesses and then pouncing on their returns for easy winners. It is a style of play she uses to this day. "If you give me a short shot, I will attack you," she says. "I try to get the point over with."

Soon Serena was beating everyone in sight, too. She also could give Venus a run for her money. Serena had the advantage of practicing against a slightly more advanced "version" of herself, which helped her improve. And as Serena improved, Venus had to come up with new ways to maintain her advantage, so she got better, too. Parents who watched helplessly as the Williams sisters blew their kids off the court liked to believe that the girls from Compton could not get any better.

They had no idea how good they would become.

Soon Venus had become a celebrity. She was featured in publications ranging from *Sports Illustrated for Kids* to *The New York Times*. Richard Williams began noticing people at her matches who did not look like parents. They were sports agents and representatives of equipment companies. Convinced that his daughter was the real deal, they started to approach him with offers of cars and houses and more money than he had ever imagined. He turned them all down—accepting these offers would mean losing control of Venus's career, and Richard was not ready for that.

Some members of the tennis world were excited about all the interest in Venus. The sport, they felt, needed to better reflect the ethnic diversity of the planet. Others cringed when they thought of children being offered $100,000 endorsement deals. How young, they asked, was *too* young?

Did You Know?

When Venus was nine, she got to hit with tennis legend John McEnroe. When she left the court, she told her father she thought she could beat him!

Heading East

chapter 3 }

> *"I hope they're less concerned with creating a champion than they are with creating a champion person."*
> — TENNIS STAR ZINA GARRISON

Richard and Oracene Williams continued to turn down every offer that came their way. For this they were applauded. But that is not to say that tennis people agreed with their methods. The United States Tennis Association (USTA) felt that Venus and Serena would soon need top-level instruction in order to keep improving. The USTA offered to enroll the girls in its Southern California program, which ranks among the world's finest. There they would be exposed to excellent coaching and compete against the best junior players on a daily basis. Richard agreed to enter his daughters in USTA junior tournaments, but declined the USTA's offer of coaching.

Venus and Serena had done wonderfully under his instruction, so he saw no reason to turn them over to strangers. He also believed that letting them practice with other youngsters would impede their progress rather than accelerate it. In each other, Richard

Venus, pictured here conducting a clinic in Washington, D.C., at age 14, has been giving back to her sport since her early teens.

reasoned, Venus and Serena had all the competition they would ever need. He also predicted they would "revolutionize" women's tennis. In the eyes of many, he was becoming the worst kind of tennis parent; he appeared to be jeopardizing the future of his children to make himself feel more important.

What critics of the Williams family did not realize was that Venus and Serena were the daughters of loving, caring parents. Richard and Oracene made rules to shield the girls from the pressures of superstardom. For example, no one was allowed to answer the phone before 10 o'clock in the morning. This ensured quiet time for the family during breakfast. If Richard or Oracene sensed that tennis was becoming too great a focus, they would simply take the racket away and say forget about playing for a while. This kept Venus and Serena from burning out.

"There's no question Venus is going to be a great player."
LINDSAY DAVENPORT

The most important rule was that tennis was never to come between the girls and their schoolwork. Richard made sure Venus and Serena knew that professional tennis would occupy only a short period of their lives, and that being an intelligent, well-rounded person had to come first. "What do you do when you leave tennis?" he would ask them. "Assuming you live until you're 75, you've got 50 years to be a fool."

As a result, Venus and Serena were straight-A students. And long before they became professional tennis players, they talked about the exciting jobs that awaited them *after* tennis. To this day, Serena teases Venus because her older sister often talked about becoming an astronaut!

The girls also received some important lessons about life through their mother's religion. A Jehovah's Witness, Oracene Williams went door-to-door to share her beliefs with others. Often, she took her daughters along. Serena remembers a lot of doors being slammed in their faces. She says this helped them realize that you cannot take that kind of thing personally.

Did You Know?

The street gangs of Compton were so proud of Venus and Serena that they agreed to a "ceasefire" whenever the girls were practicing.

In 1991, Venus was the top 12-and-under player in Southern California, and Serena was the region's highest-ranked 10-year-old. The time had now arrived, Richard decided,

Teen star Jennifer Capriati, who burned brightly then burned out.

Teen star Jennifer Capriati, who burned brightly then burned out.

for his daughters to learn from the experienced hand of a professional instructor. He collected information from all of the top coaches in the country, then chose Rick Macci, who ran a tennis school in Delray Beach, Florida. The family packed its bags and moved 3,000 miles (4,800 km) to the Sunshine State.

Although teaching Venus and Serena would now be Macci's responsibility, Richard still had a firm grasp on their careers. He pulled the girls off the junior circuit, and asked Macci to make sure they only hit with players who were better than them—which usually meant adult male instructors.

The USTA howled its disapproval. The association insisted that Venus and Serena compete in junior tournaments, so that they would be used to the pressure of big events once they turned pro. Richard responded that he thought they would grow more as players if they did *not* feel that kind of pressure at a young age. He pointed to Jennifer Capriati, who was pushed too fast and too far by her coaches and parents, and then self-destructed by the age of 16. Richard also ignored the USTA's suggestion that his daughters spend as much time as possible playing or practicing tennis. He told Macci that Venus and Serena were to spend as much time off the court as on it.

Did You Know?

Venus and Serena are both interested in pursuing careers in fashion design— a passion that first developed during their pre-teen years. Venus also thought about becoming an architect, while Serena dreamed of going to veterinary school.

Macci went along with the plan, although he did not always agree with it. Many times, he recalls, the girls would be in his office studying when he felt they should be out on the court. Sometimes they practiced less than an hour a day! And if their grades slipped, watch out— Richard would call off practice altogether.

Education was always concern number one, and the Williamses were never satisfied. Indeed, during their 18 months at Macci's, Venus and Serena attended Carver Middle School, The Driftwood Academy, and even received home schooling from Oracene for a while.

Under Macci, Venus blossomed into a world-class player. Between playing against her sister and the various teaching pros Macci provided, she could hold her own against any type of opponent. The one question that remained was whether her years away from tournament play had helped or hindered her ability to deal with the emotional challenges she would encounter as a pro. Four months after Venus's 14th birthday, everyone decided it was time to find out.

In the fall of 1994, Venus declared herself a professional and entered her first Women's Tennis Association (WTA) tournament, in Oakland, California.

Tennis coach Rick Macci

Hitting the Tour

chapter 4

"I think I can change the game."

— VENUS WILLIAMS

A week before they were to arrive in Oakland, Richard Williams ignored Rick Macci's advice and took the entire family on a trip to Disney World. Venus's coach pleaded with her dad not to go, insisting that she needed more fine tuning. But go they did, and everyone had a grand time. Venus concentrated on one thing: having fun. When she arrived in Oakland, her mind was clear and her body relaxed. She calmly prepared for her big debut, which was scheduled for October 31, Halloween.

"I like everything that I am. My mom always says, 'Can't you find something you don't like about yourself?' Actually, I can't. That's just the way I've always been."
VENUS WILLIAMS

When Venus walked on the court for her opening-round match with Shaun Stafford, the crowd must have thought they were seeing an elaborate trick-or-treat gag. Venus stood 6 feet (183 cm) tall, with long arms and legs that tensed and rippled as she moved about. Her hair was an explosion of colorful beadwork that cascaded down the sides of her beaming face. As Venus warmed up, all eyes were on her towering form as she crushed shot after shot with no apparent effort.

When the match started, Venus unveiled a booming serve, which completely handcuffed Stafford. When her opponent managed a return, Venus would flash to the net for an easy put-away. Everyone marveled at her ability to anticipate and cover the court, and also how quickly she adjusted to Stafford's desperate attempts to alter the pace of points. Venus won in straight sets, 6–3 and 6–4.

In her next match, Venus encountered the craftiest player on

Serena developed a steady game playing her sister.

the pro tour, Spain's Arantxa Sanchez Vicario. Nearly a foot shorter than Venus, she nonetheless moved just as fast and could hit any kind of shot from anywhere on the court. Venus stunned the crowd by winning the first set and taking a 3–0 lead in the second set. But Sanchez Vicario—at the time ranked second in the world—had collected a lot of information about her young opponent, and now she started to use it. She began to mess up Venus's footwork and timing by making sure she never got the ball she was expecting. Soon, the confused 14-year-old was hitting balls into the net and past the baseline. Experience won out over sheer power, as Sanchez Vicario swept the remaining 12 games and defeated Venus two sets to one.

It was back to the drawing board for Venus. Over the next two years, she entered just eight more events. Most of her time was spent practicing and playing against Serena, who was blossoming into a top player in her own right. Though smaller and less athletic than her sister, Serena had smoother strokes and was a more controlled and precise competitor. She also was quite good at changing strategy in the middle of a match when she spotted an opportunity developing.

This quality served Serena well against Venus, who was often content to slam away at her sister until she gave in. By learning how to bend without breaking, however, Serena began winning the occasional match—and developing the style that would one day define her as a pro.

The Williams File

VENUS'S FAVORITE...

Song	Twist and Shout
Flower	Carnation
Musical Group	Hole
Tennis Player	Pete Sampras
Place	The back row of a bookstore

SERENA'S FAVORITE...

Author	Maya Angelou
Instrument	Guitar
Athlete	Kobe Bryant
Place to visit	Indian Wells, CA
Fantasy	Joining the World Wrestling Federation

Sister Act

chapter 5

"If they stay healthy, there may be no stopping either of them."

—TENNIS STAR PAM SHRIVER

During 1995 and 1996, Venus and Serena Williams were hardly heard from. They stayed out of the spotlight, concentrating on their schoolwork and on their tennis. The Williams family, however, was very much the center of attention in tennis. Richard and Oracene had said on many occasions that parents who let their young teenage children compete professionally "should be shot." But when they let Venus turn pro at 14—just months before the WTA instituted a new minimum-age rule—it sure looked as if Mom and Dad were not "practicing what they preached."

More criticism was leveled at the Williamses when Venus signed a monster endorsement deal with Reebok. Some charged that their plan all along was to cash in on the success of Venus, and this was proof of it. Richard responded that neither he nor his wife was on the family's payroll, and that he had already hired experts to advise Venus and her sister on future financial matters.

Serena stretches prior to a practice session with her sister. Their parents drew much criticism for letting the girls join the WTA Tour so young.

"*So many minorities think there's only basketball and football. Now they have these girls doing their thing. I stay glued to the TV when they're playing.*"

NBA STAR KOBE BRYANT

The girls finally hit the WTA Tour for good in 1997. Venus was the first to make a splash, at one of the sport's most prestigious tournaments, the Evert Cup in Indian Wells, California. Because she was ranked 211 in the world, Venus had to play two qualifying matches just to be included in the main draw. She won both, and then proceeded to beat Iva Majoli, an exceptional player who was ranked ninth in the world. It was only Venus's 24th match as a pro, and already she had defeated her first Top 10 player. Against another Top 10 opponent, Lindsay Davenport, Venus nearly won again.

For a while, Venus Williams was all the tennis world wanted to talk about. But the noise died down as the summer wore on and other young stars began to emerge. Slowly and quietly, Venus was discovering things about life as a pro, trying to cope with the travel and the fans and the reporters, and then still perform well on the court. It was a learning summer for the 16-year-old, who hoped to apply her lessons at the U.S. Open in New York. By this time, Venus had clawed her way up the rankings to number 66.

The U.S. Open is the most important tournament in American tennis. It is not a place where a 66th-ranked teenager is likely to leave her mark. But suddenly, every part of Venus's game started to

Venus signs autographs for her fans at a 1995 event.

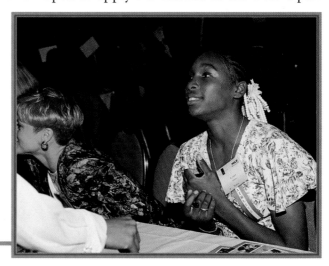

come together. Her serve was overwhelming. Her play around the net was nearly flawless. She mixed her powerful balls with tricky touch shots that messed up her opponents. It was one of the most remarkable performances anyone could remember. One player after another fell to Venus, and before anyone knew it, she was just a match away from her first "Grand Slam" final.

In an unforgettable semifinal encounter, Venus and Irina Spirlea went toe-to-toe for three incredible sets. Spirlea tried every trick she knew to unnerve her young foe, and appeared to purposely bump Venus when they changed sides during the final set. Or did Venus bump her? It seemed each player was trying to intimidate the other.

Irina Spirlea, Venus's semifinal opponent at the 1997 U.S. Open.

It was a thrilling, take-no-prisoners battle. Twice Venus faced match point, but saved it both times. Finally, she won it in a sensational, third-set tiebreaker.

Venus handled herself beautifully in the press conference that followed the match. She was charming and honest and truly excited about the opportunity to play top-ranked Martina Hingis in the final. When reporters asked if Venus felt the bumping

23

incident was racially motivated, she said no. She seemed surprised that anyone would even bother to ask such a question.

Richard Williams was a different matter. He claimed that both of his daughters had faced prejudice on the pro tour because they were black, and said Spirlea was a "big tall white turkey." This put Venus in an impossible spot. How was she supposed to prepare for the biggest match of her life while trying to respond to the endless questions that were now being posed to her about her father's remarks? Worse, those who believed Venus had done the bumping were now calling her a bully. "It was really unfair," she remembers. "It gave fans a false picture of what Serena and I are about. We're really fun and don't do bad things."

Venus tried her best to focus on her match against Hingis. A teenager herself, Hingis was on an incredible roll. She had won 62 of her last 64 matches, including the finals of the Australian Open and Wimbledon. When the match began, it was clear that the craziness had gotten to Venus. She seemed distracted and did not react well to Hingis's shots. Venus tried

Venus eyes a Martina Hingis lob during the 1997 U.S. Open final.

Although reaching the final of a Grand Slam was a great thrill, losing to Martina Hingis (left) made it hard for Venus to smile.

to get everything back over the net until her "A-game" returned, but it never did. Hingis ran her back and forth and swept the first set 6–0. Venus did better in the second set, but lost it 6–4. Hingis was the U.S. Open champion.

After the match, reporters seemed less interested in Venus's performance than in her father's comments. *Was* Spirlea a racist? *Did* Venus experience prejudice on the tour? Venus never lost her cool. She told the press she was disappointed that they would ask such questions in the same year that the tournament's main stadium was dedicated to the African-American tennis pioneer, Arthur Ashe. She said that tennis was trying to reach out to everyone, and that they were spoiling the mood.

Enter Serena

chapter 6

"Was I right or was I just crazy?
The way things are going Venus
and Serena are going to be number
one and number two in the world."

— RICHARD WILLIAMS

The 1997 season brought more surprises from the Williams clan. A few weeks after Venus's remarkable run at the U.S. Open, Serena made the WTA's Top 500 rankings for the first time, at number 453. Then, in just her fifth pro tournament, she made a big splash of her own. In back-to-back matches during an indoor event in Chicago, Serena beat Mary Pierce *and* Monica Seles, two of the best players on the tour. This amazing performance helped Serena surge more than 350 places into the WTA's Top 100 by season's end.

Venus opened the 1998 campaign with a first-round win over Martina Hingis in Sydney, Australia. It was sweet revenge for her loss to Hingis in New York. Later that spring, Venus won her first pro singles title in Oklahoma City, Oklahoma. She won two more singles crowns in 1998, and both of them were huge: the Lipton Championship

Venus beams after defeating Anna Kournikova (left) to win the 1998 Lipton Championship.

and the Grand Slam Cup. Venus collected over $1 million in prize money, placing fourth among all players, and she was one of just six players to win 50 matches during the 1998 season. At one point she reached number five in the WTA world rankings. Only two other players in history had climbed so fast so quickly. Another highlight in 1998 occurred during a match against Mary Pierce in Zurich, Switzerland. Venus squeezed out an ace that hit 127 mph on the radar gun—the fastest ever in women's tennis.

In the season's four most important tournaments—the United States, Australian, and French Opens, and Wimbledon—Venus got good results. She played with poise and maturity in the Australian and French, but came apart during Wimbledon when a few close calls went against her. She made up for this in the U.S. Open, where she reached the semifinals before bowing out.

Serena came into her own in 1998, beating three Top 10 opponents.

Serena, meanwhile, showed that her victories in Chicago were just a preview of things to come. She beat three more Top 10 players in 1998, achieving this milestone faster than anyone ever had. Her finest moment came against powerful Lindsay Davenport. The third-ranked player in the world was leading 5–2 in the second set, needing just four points to slam the door on Serena. But Serena had noticed a flaw in Davenport's game, and she began to work on her opponent. Before Davenport knew what hit her, Serena was back in the match—and eventually won the second and third sets to score a huge upset. The victory catapulted her more than 40 spots in the rankings.

In Serena's next tournament, the Australian Open, she played Venus's "old friend," Irina Spirlea. Using a scouting report supplied by her sister, Serena crushed the Romanian with ease. This set up a second-round match between Serena and Venus. It was the first time they had faced each other as pros. Venus won this meeting, and took the next one when they faced off that spring at the Italian Open.

Lindsay Davenport, who was beaten by Serena early in 1998.

"They represent a new generation of young women who are not ashamed to say what they want and go after it. In past generations, we let our rackets do the talking. But if Venus and Serena can back up their comments with results, then all the power to them. They certainly have the qualities and talent to be champions. And they seem to love the game and competing in the arena. They make it seem like it's all fun. And that's what the game should be, fun."

ALL-TIME GREAT BILLIE JEAN KING

Serena proved to be a very versatile player during her first full year on the tour. She won her first match on clay against 12th-ranked Nathalie Tauziat, and won her first time playing on grass, beating 17th-ranked Ai Sugiyama. Serena was voted the WTA's Most Impressive Newcomer in 1998—an award her sister had won the year before—and she was also named Rookie of the Year. She ended the season in the Top 20.

The Williams sisters took over the cover of Sports Illustrated for Kids *in the summer of 1998.*

Double Trouble

chapter 7

"We're showing that we're capable of doing what we said we always would."

— VENUS WILLIAMS

Not surprisingly, the Williams sisters enjoyed their greatest success in 1998 as a team. Four times during the year they won doubles titles. They also did well as members of mixed doubles teams. The family got its first two Grand Slam championships when Venus teamed with Jason Gimelstob to win the Australian and French Opens. They defeated Serena and her partner, Luis Lobo, in the French final. Serena captured the family's third and fourth Grand Slam crowns, teaming up with with Max Mirnyi to win mixed doubles championships at Wimbledon and the U.S. Open.

As the 1999 season began, Venus and Serena Williams hoped to close out the millennium as the top two singles players in women's tennis. They told anyone who would listen that '99 would be their year. At the tour's first major stop, the Australian Open, Venus bragged that her sister was "the most dangerous unseeded player ever to compete in any draw." She felt pretty stupid, however, when Serena blew a pair of match points

Serena's first Grand Slam title came as part of a mixed doubles team, with Max Mirnyi, at the 1998 U.S. Open.

and lost to unknown Sandrine Testud. And she was totally embarrassed after she failed to survive the quarterfinals. This did not make sense. Something was not right.

Richard and Oracene knew what the problem was: Their daughters were distracting each other during tournaments. They spent so much time talking about each other and hanging out together that they were losing their focus. The solution? Redo Venus's and Serena's schedules so that they would only appear in the same event a handful of times during the year.

The strategy paid off right away. In late February, Venus traveled to Oklahoma City to defend her 1998 crown in the 1999 IGA Superthrift Classic. Serena

Did You Know?

It had been over 100 years since sisters had faced each other in the finals of a major tennis event. In 1884, Maud Watson beat her older sibling, Lilian, for the Wimbledon title.

Whose trading cards will be more valuable? That's for Venus and Serena—and their fans—to decide!

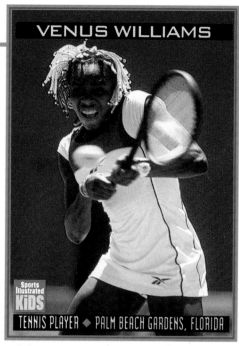

VENUS WILLIAMS

TENNIS PLAYER ◆ PALM BEACH GARDENS, FLORIDA

flew to Paris for the Gas de France. Each played marvelously throughout the week, and on the morning of March 1 they awoke to find themselves in identical positions: They were both in the finals with a chance to make history. Never had two sisters won different pro singles championships on the same day.

Serena took on Amelie Mauresmo, a native of France playing in front of her hometown fans. Serena was very nervous; she had never advanced this far before in singles. The match was a slugfest, with both players swinging as hard as they could. At one set apiece, Serena took what appeared to be a commanding 4–1 lead. But she could not close out Mauresmo, who won the next four games to go up 5–4. Facing elimination, Serena battled back to force a tiebreaker,

SERENA WILLIAMS

TENNIS PLAYER ◆ PALM BEACH GARDENS, FLORIDA

and then produced a flurry of winners to steal the match. She was glad to get her first career singles victory early in the year. "It's good to get a smaller tournament under your belt," she believes, "so that by the time you get to the Slams, you have a lot of experience."

An ocean away, Venus was thrilled to hear that her sister had won. Now it was her turn. Venus polished off Amanda Coetzer in just 58 minutes. "I found out that she won before I came out to play the match," remembers Venus, "so I really felt that it was my duty to come out and win."

A month later, the sisters made the finals again, only this time they were facing each *other* in the same tournament, the prestigious Lipton

Serena (left) and Venus exchange glances after the 1999 Lipton final.

Championships. Venus had beaten Jana Novotna and Steffi Graf. Serena, who had won the Evert Cup the previous week at Indian Wells, reached the finals by defeating top-ranked Martina Hingis and third-ranked Monica Seles.

The city of Miami was abuzz on the morning of the final. The last time two sisters had met for the singles championship of a major tournament, Miami did not even exist! The entire family was in the stands for the historic event, and as usual Richard took the opportunity to draw attention to himself. During the match, he held up a big sign that read "Welcome to the Williams Show!!"

What the crowd witnessed that day was not very pretty. It was like the old days—an all-out "nuclear war" between two sisters. Each took wild chances and tried to intimidate the other. The match featured dozens of spectacular winners, but more than 100 unforced errors as Venus and Serena tried to blow each other off the court. When the dust settled, it was Venus who had won again. "When you play an opponent who knows exactly what you're going to do, it's going to be tough," says Serena of her third loss to Venus as a pro. Was she angry? "Family comes first, no matter how many times we play each other. Nothing will come between me and my sister."

Now it was Venus who took her game to another level. In the weeks that followed, she won her first singles title on clay at the Hamburg Open in Germany. Two weeks later she won another tournament on clay, the Italian Open. The experts were impressed; this slow surface does not suit her game, so she had to make some difficult adjustments to win.

Did You Know?

Venus and Serena are the first sisters to achieve Top 10 rankings since Manuela and Katerina Maleeva did it in 1991.

Then, as suddenly as they had heated up, the Williams sisters cooled off. Although they teamed up to win the French Open doubles, in singles neither made it past the quarterfinals at the French Open or Wimbledon. They were learning how hard it was to maintain a high standard of play on the pro tour. Part of the problem was all the traveling and other demands on their time. Also, the other players were learning how to beat them. As in all sports, staying at the top of tennis often means adjusting to the adjustments your opponents make. And this did not come easily for the girls, who were only good at adjusting to each other.

The mounting losses chipped away at Venus's confidence. Often, she found herself playing defensively instead of forcing the action. This was not her game, and she knew it. Serena's problem seemed to be that she would lose her concentration during stretches of a match. This she could hardly afford. On the women's tour, the difference in skill between a player in the Top 20 and one ranked 50th or 100th is very small. What separates them is their ability to bear down and focus at key moments. This had always been one of Serena's strengths. She knew that, as the U.S. Open approached, she had better get her act together.

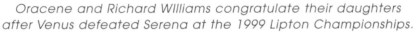

Oracene and Richard Williams congratulate their daughters after Venus defeated Serena at the 1999 Lipton Championships.

Suddenly Serena

chapter 8

"There were a lot of people who said a Williams sister would never win a Slam. Well, we plan on winning several."

— SERENA WILLIAMS

here is an unwritten rule in sports that says you do not brag about something until *after* you have done it. If you predict you will win, it gives opponents a huge incentive to beat you. That was why the mood at the 1999 U.S. Open seemed so tense. Venus and Serena Williams had worked the kinks out of their games during August and were confident they would meet in the final. And as usual, they were not afraid to say so.

This put all the other players on edge. Instead of asking how they thought they would do at the Open, reporters were now asking how they would do against Venus and Serena. Most of the players dodged this question, but in the days leading up to the tournament, a "war of words" developed between the Williams sisters and top-ranked Martina Hingis, who was favored to win the championship.

Hingis was tired of answering questions about Venus and Serena. At one point she lost her temper and told reporters that everyone in the Williams family had "a big mouth." Serena returned the blast with one of her own: She implied that Hingis was stupid, saying it was too bad she never had "a formal education." Sensing that his

Martina Hingis steals the spotlight from Richard WIlliams at the 1999 U.S. Open.

daughters might lose their focus, Richard Williams stepped in and played the role of peacemaker. He announced that he loved Martina, and that the thing he most wanted was her autograph. She responded by presenting him with a signed T-shirt and planting a big kiss on his cheek while a hundred photographers snapped their picture.

With their minds back on tennis, the Williams sisters advanced to the quarterfinals with ease. Venus defeated Barbara Schett in straight sets to earn a trip to the semifinals. Serena, meanwhile, required three sets to get past Monica Seles. Serena needed all of her quickness and anticipation to beat Seles, who rocketed shots all over the court. After the match Serena told reporters that she felt she could win the tournament—if she could play as well as she had versus Seles, no one, she predicted, would be able to beat her.

Lindsay Davenport, the world's second-ranked player, was Serena's opponent in the semifinals. One of the few players on the tour bigger and stronger than Serena, Davenport hoped to simply overpower the younger Williams sister. But all those years battling Venus had taught Serena some lessons about surviving these situations.

Davenport came out pounding the ball. Serena refused to go on the defensive, smashing Davenport's deep drives right back at her. When a few breaks went against Davenport, she lost her cool for a couple of games and Serena stole the first set. Davenport served her way back into the match and took the second set, but in the end

Serena blasts a two-handed backhand during the U.S. Open final.

it was Serena who had enough left in her tank to win.

Suddenly Serena—the "other" Williams sister—was looking like the better Williams sister. Earlier that day, Venus had dueled for three exhausting sets with Hingis and lost. It all came down to a few crucial points. Hingis made the big shots when she had to, and Venus did not. It was the biggest disappointment of her career. It had long been her dream to play Serena in the final of the U.S. Open. "I've never seen her that down before," confirms Serena.

To her credit, Venus handled the loss like a seasoned pro. When reporters offered that Hingis had made some lucky shots, Venus quickly corrected them. The better player had won that day, she said. "It wasn't luck that Martina won the match," Venus remembers. "It was hard work. I don't believe things happen because the wind blows and luck just lands on you."

Although the dream of playing Venus in the U.S. Open final had died, Serena's chances for a championship had drastically improved. In fighting so hard, Venus had "softened up" Hingis for her sister. This was clear from the start of the match—Hingis did not have her usual zip, while Serena was in full command of her game. She hammered relentlessly at Hingis with booming serves and heavy, penetrating shots from the baseline. The first set went to Serena, 6–3. The second was closer, but Serena prevailed in the tiebreaker. She shrieked with joy after winning match point, then tears streamed down her cheeks. "I thought, 'Should I scream, should I yell,

Did You Know?

Serena's win at the U.S. Open was the first by an African-American since Arthur Ashe won in 1968.

Serena and runner-up
Martina Hingis after their
clash in the U.S. Open.

or should I cry?" Serena recalls. "I guess I ended up doing them all!"

Serena had little time to savor her victory. She and Venus had also made the finals of the women's doubles, and they were scheduled to play Chanda Rubin and Sandrine Testud later that day. It took an entire set for Serena to refocus and for Venus to perk up; by the time they were ready to play, the sisters were already down a set. After that, however, it was all Venus and Serena. They wiped out Rubin and Testud in the next two sets for another Grand Slam title.

The 1999 season held one more special treat for fans of the Williams sisters. In the final of the Grand Slam Cup in Munich, Germany, Venus and Serena faced each other again. In a hard-fought match, Serena finally got a win against Venus. "She knew eventually I would take a match from her," Serena laughs.

Venus finished the year ranked third, while Serena was right behind her in fourth place. Between tournament winnings and endorsement deals, the sisters collected just under $10 million. Although they did not finish the year one-two, it was not a bad way to end the millennium!

"I know Venus was sad when she didn't get to the final, but she was happy I won."

SERENA WILLIAMS

Rowdy Richard

chapter 9

> *"I try to keep the pressure off so that they will always enjoy the game and think of it as fun."*
>
> — RICHARD WILLIAMS

How good can Venus and Serena Williams be? Some believe this depends on how "bad" their father gets. Richard Williams is the most talked-about man in tennis these days, and most of what people are saying is not very nice. No one doubts that Richard loves his daughters. Still, Venus and Serena often find themselves having to explain his behavior instead of thinking about their tennis.

Some believe that Richard Williams is good for the girls. He sees when they are feeling stress, and those are the times he tries to focus attention on himself. The higher the stakes, he claims, the more outrageous he gets. Whether or not this is true is a matter of some debate.

As Richard sees it, his conduct at tournaments is hardly worth discussing. His primary goal has always been to provide a loving, stable home for his daughters. And as he and Oracene are proud to point out, all five Williams girls are happy, mature, and successful.

Is Richard bad for tennis? That depends on which side of the sport you stand.

Father Figure

"Nobody knows those girls better than their parents. The road they've gone on couldn't have been better selected."
TENNIS COACH NICK BOLLETTIERI

"Mr. Williams has a lot of common sense, and it's obvious that he is devoted to his children."
TENNIS LEGEND ARTHUR ASHE

"I think they would benefit with a tennis coach, somebody who's been there. But I wouldn't underestimate them. They've surprised the tennis world."
ALL-TIME GREAT CHRIS EVERT

"Free of shame, he is also free to love his highly profitable girls wholeheartedly, which—it is clear for all to see—he does."
TIME MAGAZINE COLUMNIST ROGER ROSENBLATT

By pulling Venus and Serena out of junior competition, he thumbed his nose at the USTA, which has been running the sport in America for a very long time. If every father got it in his head that his daughters would be harmed by the USTA instead of helped, the result would be chaos in the junior ranks.

On the other hand, if Richard Williams was trying to shield his daughters from the negative experiences they might face in a sport that is still run and played mostly by white Americans, then he might have been right to do what he did. The success that Venus and Serena have enjoyed despite challenging the system has sent a very strong message to those who control tennis in the United States. The sport needs to look itself in the mirror and see that its face is no longer the face of America. Only then will it be able to truly reach out to people of all races and attract its fair share of the wonderful athletes this country produces.

Whether he is good, bad, or something in between, Richard Williams has accomplished what many in the old neighborhood thought would be impossible. He and Oracene produced two well-adjusted, world-class tennis players under conditions that were far less than favorable. Theirs was one of the dreams that did not die in Compton. And for that they deserve more credit than they will probably ever receive.

"All my career I've had people ask when I was going to get a real coach. Now, hopefully, people will see that our parents knew what they were doing."

VENUS WILLIAMS

Who's Better?

chapter 10

"They're totally different players, but the common thread is both will run over glass to hit a shot."

— FORMER COACH, RICK MACCI

When you ask Venus who the better Williams sister is, she points to Serena. Ask Serena and she will tell you it is Venus. That is how much love and respect the girls have for each other. What is the truth? Their games are still developing, so it is difficult to say.

Until Serena won the 1999 U.S. Open, most fans assumed that Venus was the superstar in the family. A look at her game shows why. She whips her 6-foot (183-cm) 170-pound (77-kg) frame into every shot with maximum force, hitting her forehands and backhands hard, and placing them very close to the baseline. This pins opponents back and forces them to hit defensive shots. When Venus sees a weak return, she uses her long arms and giant strides to move quickly toward the net for a put-away.

Venus puts everything she has into her shots.

These were the skills that helped Venus win her first Grand Slam singles title at Wimbledon in 2000. Her speed really came into play on the super-fast grass surface. Opponents hit sure winners only to watch in frustration as she ran them down to keep the points alive.

Venus's opponents can look forward to more frustration, as she learns more and more about the game. Already, she can change the amount of topspin she puts on her forehand and has learned how to disguise her shots. She also is changing the pace and location on her groundstrokes and serves in order to mess up an opponent's timing and conserve her own energy during a match. In short, Venus appears to be the kind of intelligent and athletic player who should be able to dominate her sport.

Of course, Serena will have something to say about that. Though smaller than her sister, Serena is equally athletic and slightly more consistent with her groundstrokes. She is also *meaner*. Venus smiles a lot during matches. Serena does not. And she has a memory like an elephant—she never forgets anything an opponent does to her.

Serena hits her forehands, backhands, and volleys with the same force as Venus, and may soon match her sister's serve. She already can match Venus's remarkable strength and stamina thanks to a weight training regimen she began in 1998.

Venus Williams

YEAR	ACHIEVEMENT
2000	Singles Champion and Doubles Champion (with Serena), Wimbledon
1999	Singles Champion, Italian Open
1999	Doubles Champion, U.S. Open (with Serena)
1999	Doubles Champion, French Open (with Serena)
1998	Singles Champion, Grand Slam Cup
1998	Mixed Doubles Champion, French Open
1998	Mixed Doubles Champion, Australian Open

Serena Williams

2000	Doubles Champion (with Venus), Wimbledon
1999	Singles Champion, U.S. Open
1999	Doubles Champion, U.S. Open (with Venus)
1999	Doubles Champion, French Open (with Venus)
1998	Mixed Doubles Champion, Wimbledon
1998	Mixed Doubles Champion, U.S. Open

As for Serena's court sense and anticipation, they are excellent after so many years chasing down her sister's shots. Serena has also learned how to spot the slightest flaw in an opponent's game and turn it to her advantage. This quality has a lot of tennis people excited. It is one thing to know a player's weaknesses before a match and then exploit them. It is something very different to notice when an opponent's best shots are not clicking, and then to be brave enough

Serena searches for flaws in an enemy's game.

"I think Venus is the best athlete the women's game has seen so far."
ANDRE AGASSI

to feed her those balls on purpose. Indeed, Serena is at her most devilish when she plays to an opponent's "strengths."

Alas, the answer to "Who's better?" is still in the eye of the beholder. Each sister now owns a Grand Slam singles title. Venus has a slight edge in the physical department, while Serena seems to have a better idea of what it takes to win. You get the feeling, though, that this question will be answered again and again over the next few years—on the tennis court, in front of millions of fans, with millions of dollars on the line.

You also get the feeling that, once the first shot is struck, none of that will matter. It will be like the old days—just two sisters, playing on the cracked asphalt, with passion, pride, and the love of their parents fueling their thirst for victory.

Or, as Serena still calls it, "nuclear war."

It is difficult to tell who won the 1999 Grand Slam Cup from this picture.
Serena's fans know that it was her first win against Venus as a pro.

Index